TOTAL STICK FIGHTING
SHINTAIDO BOJUTSU

TOTAL STICK FIGHTING
SHINTAIDO BOJUTSU

Hiroyuki Aoki

KODANSHA INTERNATIONAL
Tokyo • New York • London

NOTE: The diagrams shown on page 33 are reprinted from *Shintaido: The Body Is a Message of the Universe* by Hiroyuki Aoki (San Francisco: Shintaido of America, 1982).

Front jacket photo by BAB Japan. Back jacket photo by Naoto Suzuki. Most interior photos by Taro Aoki.

All calligraphy by Hiroyuki Aoki.

Distributed in the United States by Kodansha America, Inc., 575 Lexington Avenue, New York, NY 10022, and in the United Kingdom and continental Europe by Kodansha Europe Ltd., 95 Aldwych, London WC2B 4JF.

Published by Kodansha International Ltd., 17-14 Otowa 1-chome, Bunkyo-ku, Tokyo 112-8652 and Kodansha America, Inc.

First edition, 2000

00 01 02 03 04   10 9 8 7 6 5 4 3 2 1

ISBN 4-7700-2383-9

Library of Congress Cataloging-in-Publication Data

Aoki, Hiroyuki.
    Total stick fighting: shintaido bojutsu / Hiroyuki Aoki.-- 1st ed.
      p. cm.
    ISBN 4770023839 (hardcover)
     1. Stick fighting. I. Title.

GV1141 .A65 2000

CONTENTS

FOREWORD

I am sure that anyone who is familiar with Shintaido will rejoice at the publication of this long-awaited "definitive word" on Shintaido bojutsu, and perhaps the start of a widespread Shintaido bojutsu movement all over the world.

I have known and studied with Master Hiroyuki Aoki for nearly thirty years. Our most recent meeting took place at a gasshuku (training retreat) in the south of France in May 1999. It was in that same country, quite some time ago, that I first began practicing Shintaido and met Aoki-sensei. Now both of us are entering our "third age," so I was happy to have the opportunity to practice with him again in France.

Our first meeting was in 1972 in Paris, and I was impressed even then with his tremendous sense of humor, because he cautioned me about the danger of breaking my ankles if I meditated too long in the formal kneeling seiza position—which was no real danger, given how painful keeping that position was for me at the time.

Since then I have attended many workshops and classes that he has taught in the United States, the United Kingdom, France, and Japan, and I have never failed to derive great benefit from his teaching, whether the subject was Shintaido honka (Shintaido's core program), kenjutsu or bojutsu. Early respect has been coupled with friendship as our relationship has evolved over the years.

I first started practicing bojutsu in 1972 or thereabouts. At the time, Shintaido bojutsu was still a "work in progress." The curriculum was fairly limited and the method of teaching, minimalist. I spent the first year practicing mochikae (the daily assignment was to do one thousand, which took about half an hour). I was then shown suihei uchi by my French instructor, who said that was to be my "homework" for the second year. Not very exciting, but for some reason I found that approach to be quite satisfying. In fact, while returning to the United States for a short stay between the two years I spent in France, I dutifully practiced mochikae at the stern of the S.S. France, which was ferrying me across the Atlantic. I'm sure the other passengers were nonplussed, but I enjoyed looking out over the ocean while completing my thousand-count routine.

I was fortunate to be studying Shintaido in Japan in the early 1980s, when Aoki-sensei began to introduce the new bojutsu program. My understanding at the time was that Aoki-sensei was disappointed that the style of physical movement he had developed in the core Shintaido program was not being translated into bojutsu, where movements remained quite stiff and rough, especially in kumibo (partner practice using the bo), resulting in quite a number of injuries to practitioners.

He told us that it was totally anachronistic to be trying to learn to use the bo as a weapon at the end of the twentieth century, and that bojutsu should instead be viewed as a discipline that would help us as we continued along our Shintaido path. From that point, instead of whacking each other with our bo, we began to throw the bo into the air, catch them and roll with them onto the ground. We would balance them on the tops of our feet, use them to play catch with a partner, and do dancelike movements in which we would move in tandem with our bo, alternately leading and following them. The ultimate goal was to establish unification, even intimacy, with the bo.

In this way we finally learned to regard the bo as a tool with which we could achieve greater flexibility in our bodies and minds, rather than as a weapon that had lost all connection to everyday life. But I felt that this approach was not essentially different from the way I had begun my own practice of bojutsu; it was just more efficient (and more fun, I admit).

During the early years, I had relatively few opportunities to practice with a partner, and so my bo became my keiko partner, so to speak. Through occasional visits from Japanese teachers I was able to learn some additional techniques, but during those early years the most important element in my practice and meditation was hitori-geiko, or solitary practice.

Instructional advancements have given practitioners today a wider range of options, but the importance of hitori-geiko cannot be overemphasized. Solitary practice may figure heavily in the training of many readers of this book, and I would like to point out that it remains as essential and beneficial as ever.

I would recommend that readers—whether they are working with a teacher or alone—be sure to allow enough time to truly assimilate the various parts of the program outlined here. Of course, the ideal would be to find a qualified bojutsu instructor and study with him or her. But if that is not feasible, why not try spending a year or so running eiko and practicing the various techniques for unification of practitioner and bo that are described in this book before moving on to specific kata. The results may surprise you.

Michael Thompson
General Instructor
Co-Founder, Shintaido of America

INTRODUCTION

On a May weekend not long ago, I had the pleasure of joining 160 people for a gasshuku (training retreat) hosted by Shintaido of France and held just outside Nice in the south of France. For three days we gathered on a grassy field, doing keiko (training) under the clearest of blue skies. A cool breeze moved in the branches of the surrounding trees and refreshed us as we trained. We did very good keiko.

At the closing ceremony I was given a set of tableware in commemoration of the retreat. Suitably, the utensils were made of olive wood, a local product and common throughout southern Europe. What particularly caught my eye among the utensils was a kind of pestle often used in French kitchens. I took it in my hands and examined it. It was shaped like a calabash, about as long as my hand and five or six centimeters in diameter.

I began to test this piece of wood, using it to tap various parts of my body. I tapped my hand and knees. I tapped my head with it lightly. It gave me a jolt that was stronger than I had expected. A person's fist, I thought, could never deliver as sharp a blow as this stick could. I realized that even a little cooking utensil like this could serve as a weapon.

Before human beings learned to craft metal tools, they most likely relied on sticks and stones to defend themselves. Even after they had learned to forge swords from copper and iron, weapons of that sort would have been very expensive, and far beyond most people's means.

So it would have been essential to keep rocks and sturdy sticks of some length at hand, in order to protect one's family and community and to hunt animals for food. As time went on, people naturally developed more and more efficient ways to wield these weapons.

Stick fighting technique, or bojutsu, has existed nearly everywhere in the world from prehistoric times. In China, for instance, martial arts developed considerably during the period from the Eastern Chou through the Warring States eras (770–221 B.C.), when many wars were fought. Refined techniques for hand-to-hand combat and bojutsu eventually spread from the continent to the Kingdom of Ryukyu (present-day Okinawa). There these fighting forms were refined over the centuries, leading to the development of karate and Ryukyu bojutsu. Later these forms were introduced to the main islands of Japan, the home of budo, the martial way.

SHINTAIDO BOJUTSU

In creating Shintaido bojutsu, I selected four of the greatest kata from among the kata that are essential to Ryukyu bojutsu and recast them completely in keeping with Shintaido philosophy. I also included one kata that I had developed. Then I broke all of these down and created the kihon waza, systematizing the techniques to make them accessible to beginners. As a natural result, the fundamental principles and philosophy of Shintaido are the core of Shintaido bojutsu.

I developed Shintaido as a way of reawakening the natural properties of the body, opening one's consciousness, freeing the spirit and creating strong bonds between people. Shintaido is a form of body work that makes it possible to realize one's true self, purify the soul and elevate the spirit. Besides bojutsu, I have created several other Shintaido martial art forms, striving in each to maintain a balance between the philosophy of Shintaido and the essence of the traditional kata. These martial art forms are jojutsu (short staff technique), karate, jujutsu (traditional grappling and throwing technique) and kenjutsu (sword technique). The end result of these intensive efforts is that we now have a complete system of Shintaido martial arts.

Shintaido bojutsu has two features that make it unique among the world's bojutsu traditions. First, as I have mentioned, it is in its essence Shintaido—intended to reawaken the body to its own natural properties, open up the consciousness and set the spirit free. Second, it is unique in that it includes nagewaza (throwing techniques).

The inclusion of nagewaza was a late development that resulted in part from a journey I made. In 1976 I felt I had finished developing the system for teaching Shintaido bojutsu, and during the next two years I traveled extensively through Central and South America. I was profoundly moved by the scale and sheer beauty of places like Mato Grosso, in Brazil, and the Andes mountains. I determined to try to create a stick-fighting system that would have something in common with the grandeur of those landscapes and at the same time be imbued with the deeply natural aspect of our humanity. With this in mind, I completely revised the Shintaido bojutsu I had developed to that point, and was able to make it into a much richer system.

I returned to Japan at the end of March 1978 and for the next month or two began having a vision every day in which a man would suddenly attack me with a bo. Each time, I would see this vision once and then it would be repeated, but the second time I would see a man step out of my body and use stick-fighting techniques that I had never seen to throw the attacker off his feet. At first all I could do was just watch. The waza were so amazing that they took my breath away. Then it occurred to me that I should be recording the techniques, so I began to take notes each time.

In all I recorded seventy-five nagewaza. For purposes of teaching, I rejected twenty-five of these throwing techniques as too difficult for regular students. I decided that the other fifty were suitable for all Shintaido students. After I had finished systematizing Shintaido bojutsu, I divided it into three areas: beginning, intermediate and advanced techniques.

Total Stick Fighting: Shintaido Bojutsu targets students at the first two of these levels. In the future I also hope to compile a text for intermediate and advanced students, as well as one for very advanced practitioners.

Work through this book gradually and at your own pace. When practicing, please remember to release all unnecessary tension from your body. Always move fluidly and gently and use only the minimum required strength.

Shintaido bojutsu is above all else a body art meant to purify the mind and soul, refine the ki and elevate the spirit by means of the extraordinarily simple tool of the bo. Through Shintaido bojutsu, I hope that you will devote yourselves to becoming more vibrant and awake. I hope that no matter what anyone else may say or do, you will continue to perform keiko while aspiring to truth and creating and maintaining harmony among heaven, nature and human society. I hope that *Total Stick Fighting: Shintaido Bojutsu* will reach everyone who desires to achieve these goals.

I would like to thank the people who helped me to produce this book. Shigeharu Suzuki was instrumental in producing and organizing the text, over a period of many months. I am very grateful to him, and to Lee Ordeman, who spent an equal amount of time painstakingly translating the text and collaborating on its revision.

Michael Thompson and Fugaku Ito of Shintaido of America and Masashi Minagawa of Shintaido of Great Britain offered invaluable assistance throughout this project. They were always available at short notice to offer advice or look at a new chapter.

Thanks are also due to Mitsuru Okada, who supervised the techniques shown in the photographs.

For their help with the translation, I would like to thank Toshimitsu Ishii, Tomoko Oka and Taro Aoki.

I am also grateful to Hiroshi Akiyama, Toshimitsu Ishii, Hideki Oi and Kosuke Suhara, who demonstrated the techniques for the photographs.

These people provided invaluable assistance, but final responsibility for any shortcomings that the text may have is my own.

Hiroyuki Aoki
February 2000

CHAPTER 1

Basic Exercises

GETTING STARTED

Use of the bo

When using a weapon as large as the bo, it is important that you really feel its weight with your body. It is also important that when you use the bo the movements of your entire body are flowing and smooth. You should not swing the bo erratically, nor should you use it to strike at someone else or at an object with excessive force.

Treatment of the bo

The best kind of material for the bo is a hardwood that has some natural give. You may want to make a bag for storing the bo; materials like vinyl that do not allow proper ventilation should be avoided.

Since the bo is long (usually about 180 centimeters) and made of wood, it will warp if stored vertically. It is best to store the bo so that it lies flat—for instance, on the floor, in a safe place along a wall. The bo should be stored in a cool, dry place, away from direct sunlight.

Building a wall rack for your bo is also a good idea. Or you can hang two cords from the wall and then, after storing the bo in its bag, use these to support it, wrapping one around each end of the bo (actually, at points about fifty centimeters from each end) so that the bo is supported evenly on the wall.

Think of the bo as a weapon. Consider its edges to be similar to the blade of a knife—always handle the bo with care. The bo should periodically be wiped down, with a towel that is first run under hot water and then thoroughly wrung out; use a firm motion when wiping the wood.

Do not straddle or step over the bo. Do not kick the bo or otherwise touch it with your foot. Do not thoughtlessly handle or touch someone else's bo.

I have designed the basic practice exercises included here to be simple and enjoyable, so that newcomers to bojutsu can become accustomed to handling the bo in as short a time as possible. These exercises may look quite simple, but they are all excellent forms of practice, because they incorporate the deepest mysteries of various schools of bojutsu. The Japanese names of some of the techniques contain an element of humor, so avoid placing too much emphasis on understanding and remembering them.

BASIC EXERCISES

Bo Taiso (Warm-up exercises)

Use of the bo allows the movements of the body to become larger and more relaxed than would be possible empty-handed. When performing bo taiso, it is essential to extend the feeling of relaxation to every part of the body, while continuing to breathe naturally.

When performing the static stretches described in this section, hold each stretch for an unhurried ten counts at least. Be careful not to overdo it. Generally speaking, if you feel pain, ease up a bit.

FULL-BODY TWISTS

1   *2*   *3*   *4*

1 Stand with your feet slightly wider than the width of your shoulders. Hold the bo lightly with an overhand grip, as shown. Relax, releasing tension gradually from your neck and shoulders on down through your torso, hips, legs and feet.
2 Thrust the bo upward, while extending your line of sight to infinity.
3–4 Hold the bo horizontally while twisting to the left and right (with the spine as the center axis).

SIDE STRETCHES

5

6

7

FORWARD AND BACK STRETCHES

8

9

5 Thrust the bo upward.

6–7 With the arms extended, bend the upper half of the body to the left and then the right, allowing the entire side of the body to stretch gradually. Use the weight of the bo to help extend the stretch.

8–9 In the same way, use the weight of the bo to stretch forward and backward. When you bend deeply in this way, your entire body, from feet to hands, should form a graceful curve. Distribute your weight evenly and bend your knees slightly, to avoid placing pressure on the lower back.

TWISTS WITH BO ON SHOULDER

10

11

12

13

14

10 Shoulder the bo.

11–12 Twist the body to the left and then to the right.

13–14 Bend forward from the hips while twisting the torso up to the left and right.

(The line of sight should follow the extension of the upper tip of the bo. It is all right to bend the knees slightly.)

15–16 Twist to the left and then to the right, while leaning backward.
17–18 Bend deeply forward and then backward. You may bend the knees slightly.
Take care not to place too much pressure on the lower back.

19

20

21

22

23

24

19–24 With the bo held in both hands and your arms extended overhead, bend at the waist and rotate your upper body deeply 360° several times. Lightly bending the knees will ease pressure on the lower back. Repeat in the opposite direction.

25   26   27

28   29   30

25–26 Rest the bo lightly on your knees, keeping your feet planted close together. Lower yourself to a squat on the balls of your feet and rise to a standing position, pausing in both positions to lightly stretch the knees. Repeat. Be careful to move smoothly between the squatting and standing positions. Stopping halfway or moving too slowly may place pressure on the knees.

27–28 Extend one leg out to the side, with the heel down and toes pointing up. Squat slightly over the other foot, spreading your koshi (hips and waist) wide and keeping your foot and bent knee aligned. Press the bo lightly to your knees, relax and hold the position.

29–30 Next, do deeper stretches. Squat all the way down over the bent leg, keeping the heel down if possible. Extend the other leg out to the opposite side. This kind of deep stretching can be difficult for beginners. If you find the deeper stretch uncomfortable, do just the shallower version at first.

Bo juggling

Bo juggling helps you develop a number of essential abilities. These include manual dexterity and sensitivity to movement of the bo as it spins and turns.

Be sure to try these exercises in both directions. Try your own variations, also.

31

32

33

34

35

36

31–33 The figure-eight. Hold the bo underhand/overhand at its center and twirl it from side to side in a weaving, horizontal figure-eight pattern, leading with the underhand end of the bo.

34–36 Twirl the bo in the same manner, but with one hand. Then try the other hand.

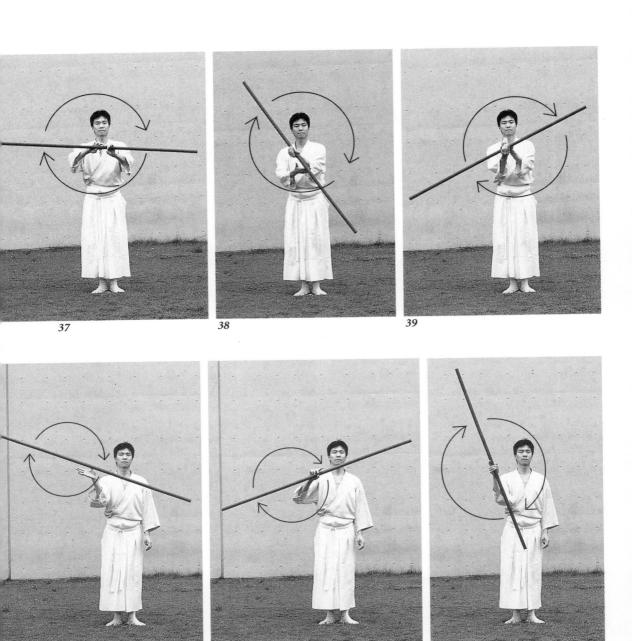

37   38   39

40   41   42

37–39 Try two-handed overhand bo spinning. Hold the bo at its center with both hands, overhand. Begin to spin the bo counterclockwise. As the bo spins, your right hand will begin to lose its grip. Simply move it under your left hand to receive the bo as it comes around. Next the left hand will be forced to let go. Turn it back to the overhand position to grasp the bo. Continue. The important thing to remember is to move repeatedly from a double overhand grip to crossing the right hand under the left.
40–42 Using one hand, spin the bo in front of the body, repeatedly releasing and catching it to maintain momentum as the bo turns. Try the other hand.

Bo balancing

These exercises involve balancing the bo on various parts of the body. First try balancing it on the end of a finger or the top of your foot, at the base of the toes. When you become accustomed to this, try balancing the bo on your shoulder, your chin, or on the tip of another bo.

43—49 "Bo balancing" done on the palm of the hand (43), the fingertip (44), the top of the foot, at the base of the toes (45), the shoulder (46), the chin (47) and the tip of another bo (48—49).

Furimawashi (Swinging the bo)

This exercise is usually done using from one to three bo at a time. Holding the bo at their extreme end, swing them back and forth around your body widely. Be sure to check beforehand that there is no one around you. Also, be careful not to let go of the bo (when your hands are sweaty, the bo can become slippery).

50 51 52

53 54 55

50–61 Furimawashi performed with two bo.

56

57

58

59

60

61

Mochikae (Switching hands)

This exercise helps you to develop ambidexterity in your handling of the bo, so that you will not drop it during kumibo (partner practice using the bo) or when you are completing a kata (set series of attack and defense movements). As you become more familiar with mochikae, you should begin to practice keeping your hands spread open so that the bo rests on the palms, rather than actually gripping the bo.

62 Hold the bo in both hands so that it is evenly supported. The arms and hands should be kept outstretched. Allow the hands to slide along the bo as it turns. **63–67** Shift the bo, turning it 180°, back and forth in a continuous rhythm.

Catch-bo

This exercise is designed to help you become accustomed to having a bo thrust at you and to help you learn to respond to the movements of your opponent without fear. At first you should practice this alone. Toss the bo up into the air, release the tension from your body, and gently catch the bo. Next, try practicing with a partner. At first, you should stand quite close to each other as you toss the bo back and forth. Later, when you become more accustomed to this, you can increase the distance to as much as twenty meters. Allow your body to relax completely as you prepare to catch the bo. Be careful to avoid injury.

68 69 70

68–70 Catch-bo performed alone is also referred to as ten-nage (throwing the bo up to heaven).

71

72

73

71–76 When you become comfortable with ten-nage, practice catch-bo with a partner.

74

75

76

Sanpo-uke (Receiving attacks from three directions) using ichimonji-uke

Ichimonji-uke is a blocking technique against an overhead attack. Its name derives from the way the bo, when it is thrust into the air, resembles the Japanese character for the numeral "one" (written as a single horizontal line). In sanpo-uke, ichimonji-uke is performed in three directions, as if to deflect attacks from the front and either side.

77

78

79

77 Grip the bo with the backs of both hands facing up, as if you were holding a set of reins.

78–79 Then either swing or thrust the bo upward into daijodan (overhead) position.

80 81

82 83

80–83 Return to the original position. Swing or thrust the bo up into left jodan (**81**; regarding jodan, see page 33). Return the bo to the original position (**82**) and swing or thrust into right daijodan (**83**). Continue, doing sanpo-uke many times, with a smooth and rhythmic motion.

Namigaeshi (Turning back waves)

This drill provides practice blocking frontal jab attacks to your upper body. Start by holding the bo overhand. Keep your knees slightly bent (refer to Figure 77).

84

85

86

87

88

89

84 To begin, place the bo in a vertical position over to one side.
84–86 Sweep broadly across to the other side.
87–89 Turn the bo over, end for end, then sweep back to the other side. Continue with a smooth, rhythmic motion.

90

91

92

93

90–93 This is a detailed view of how to turn the bo over end for end, as required in Figures 86–87.

Bo no ageoroshi (Raising and lowering the bo)

Bo no ageoroshi is a meditative exercise in which the practitioner can experience the essence of Shintaido.

94

95

94 This stage of bo no ageoroshi is known as shoko. Stand with your arms outstretched, holding the bo out by its extreme end. Extend your line of sight in the same direction as the head of the bo—beyond the horizon.

95–97 Slowly and carefully raise the bo, while continuing to extend your line of vision over the bo's tip. If clouds or a ceiling obscures your view, see beyond them. Look heavenward. This vertical stage is known as tenso.

96

97

98

99

98–99 Slowly return to the original position, shoko, and repeat.

Eiko dai (Glory)

Eiko is a fundamental movement of Shintaido; the word translates literally as "glory." Here it is done in its large-scale variation, Eiko dai.

100

101

102

103

104

105

100–101 Begin with the bo extended (shoko). Then raise the bo, stretching your whole body upward.

102–104 At the very moment that you reach the peak of the stretch, start running forward while making a long, gradual, "cosmic" cut downward with the bo. The cut and the run should be unified, from beginning to end. The distance run can vary greatly, from the length of a room to several kilometers.

105 Complete the movement with your arms and the bo extended forward in shoko.

(For more on Eiko, refer to page 194.)

Hoshi-otoshi (Making stars fall)

Hoshi-otoshi is another beneficial meditative exercise.

106

106 Hold the bo at one end and raise it up as high as possible. Then trace small circles in the air with its extended tip, as if you were stirring up the sky, trying to make stars fall from the heavens.

Irimukae (Entering and inviting)

The object of irimukae is to increase the sense of oneness that you feel with the bo.

107

108

107–108 Hold the bo as shown. First, imagine the bo melting into you. Then imagine yourself melting into the bo.

CHAPTER 2

Kihon Waza

NOTES ON KIHON WAZA

Kihon waza are basic techniques for attack and defense that can be practiced alone or in groups. These techniques are called basic because they are fundamental, not because they are particularly easy to perform. Since kata and kumibo both are built upon the kihon waza, some people tend to think that kata and kumibo are a higher level of practice, but in fact each of these three forms of practice—kihon waza, kata and kumibo—has a different objective. Each is very important and contains a kernel of the real essence of bojutsu practice. Even for the most advanced students of bojutsu, practice of kihon waza serves as the core and source for the ongoing development of his or her keiko.

This chapter uses terms such as "attack" and "jab," but these terms are intended only to express images; in fact you should be sure never to strike a person's body with your bo, as this can be very dangerous. Practice should be done using full force, but its object is for all participants to improve their abilities, not to dominate or outdo one another.

The following is a list of the simplified names of kihon waza covered in this chapter.

Uchiwaza (Striking techniques)
• Jodan uchikomi*
• Daijodan uchioroshi
• Jodan uchiharai*
• Jodan gyaku-te uchi*
• Suihei uchikomi*
• From matsukaze uchi* to suna kake 1
  —Suna kake 2

Tsukiwaza (Thrusting techniques)
• Chudan morote-zuki
• Zenshin ippon morote-zuki
• Chudan taguri-zuki
• Zenshin ippon taguri-zuki

Ukewaza (Receiving techniques)
• Gedan-barai* (with nukiotoshi)
• Kohan
• Ichimonji
• Ryuhi

* Can be used as either uchiwaza or ukewaza.

KAMAE: BASIC WAYS OF STANDING

Examples of stances

There are a number of different stances, or kamae, that are basic to the kihon waza. In all of them it's important to stand naturally and to release excess tension from your body. (For more on stances, see Appendix III.)

SAGE BO: STANDING AT REST WITH THE BO

1   2

Before beginning practice and also when at rest, stand with the bo tucked under your right arm.

1 (front view)

2 (side view)

With your legs at shoulder width and your koshi (hips and waist) slightly back, stand with your weight just forward of the arches of your feet. This is known as hachiji-dachi as well as seiritsu (formal standing position).

Grip the bo about a third of the way from its lowered front end. Keep the rear end tucked lightly under your right arm. This position is called right sage bo.

Just before using the bo, always shift it over to the same position on the left side.

YOI (READY POSITION)

3

4

3 (front view)

4 (side view)

This position is also known as yame.

Stand in musubidachi—with your feet in a V-shape, keeping your heels together and toes apart. Grip the bo in both hands, as if dividing its length approximately in thirds. Look ahead, just over your right forearm.

Before beginning kihon waza or kumibo (partner practice), make sure to hold the bo in this manner on the left side.

When you do kata on the right side, switch to the same position on the right side.

KIBA-DACHI

5

6

5 (front view)

6 (side view)

Open your stance a bit wider than your shoulders, keeping your feet parallel. With your koshi low, keep your upper body upright. Grip the bo lightly and look straight ahead, toward infinity. Align the front tip of the bo with your line of sight. With your right hand, rest the back end of the bo on your right hip. (If this way of standing proves difficult, you may want to point your toes slightly outward.)

FUDO-DACHI

7
8

7 (front view)

8 (side view)

Stand in fudo-dachi with your weight distributed evenly over both legs. One foot is forward and the other is back, pointing sideways. The knees are bent and the koshi is low. Grip the bo lightly and look straight ahead, toward infinity. Align the front tip of the bo with your line of sight. With your right hand, rest the back of the bo on your right hip.

Shift your weight forward slightly in this position for zenkutsu fudo-dachi. Shift your weight back slightly for kokutsu fudo-dachi (also referred to as kokutsu-dachi).

(See Figures 176–181 for more on fudo-dachi.)

LEVELS OF WAZA: DAN

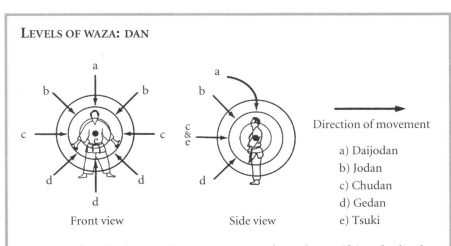

Front view

Side view

Direction of movement

a) Daijodan
b) Jodan
c) Chudan
d) Gedan
e) Tsuki

Waza are described using the waza name and words specifying the level to which the waza is applied in relation to the body. These levels, or "dan," are daijodan (overhead), jodan (upper level), chudan (middle level) and gedan (lower level). These charts show the levels of waza, as well as the placement for tsukiwaza.

Taking stances

9   10   11

12   13   14

9 Left sage bo in seiritsu (formal standing position):
Stand with your legs at shoulder width, keeping your koshi slightly back. Stand with your weight slightly forward of the arches of your feet.
10 Grip the bo with your right hand.
11–13 Rotate the back end of the bo down and through to the front.
14 Left yoi, drawing the feet together into musubidachi (heels together and toes apart).

MOVING TO FUDO-DACHI FROM YOI

15 16

17 18 19

15 Left yoi.

16 Kensei: Align the bo with your forward line of vision. Rest the back part of the bo lightly on your bent left upper arm and hold it as if you were pulling back on a bow and arrow. (If you are practicing with a partner, point the bo at his throat, to hold him in check.) This position is known as kensei. (To jab with the bo in this position, draw back on the bo and thrust forward in one flick of the wrist.)

17 Pull the bo straight back.

18–19 Left jodan uchikomi: While moving the right foot back, do uchikomi to chudan. (With your left hand, push the rear portion of the bo straight forward into chudan.)

20

21

22

20 Left fudo-dachi.

21 Draw the left foot back, next to the right (or draw the right foot up, next to the left) into musubidachi. At the same time, while drawing the front part of the bo in toward the body, raise the back part up into jodan.

22 Yame position (identical to yoi).

MOVING TO SAGE BO FROM YAME POSITION

23

24

25

26

27

28

23 Yame position.

24–25 Lower the top end of the bo, and rotate the bottom end from behind.

26–27 Tuck the bo under your left arm.

28 Move your right foot out laterally from musubidachi into seiritsu stance.

DESCRIPTIONS OF KIHON WAZA

Kihon waza are to be done on both the right and left sides, but for the sake of practicality they are shown here only as done on one side. When you practice, work on both right and left sides alternately (doing mochikae, or switching hands, in between). (In the case of tsukiwaza, do each waza on one side about ten times and then practice the other side.)

UCHIWAZA   Striking techniques

Jodan uchikomi

Uchikomi from jodan to chudan (Moving forward, fudo-dachi)

29   30

29 Left chudan stance: Stand in fudo-dachi, with the left foot forward. (If you are practicing with a partner, aim the bo at his throat.)

30 Mochikae: Swiftly rotate the bo (vertically) end for end. This involves changing grips, sliding your hands along the bo, and turning it over so that what was the front is at the back, and the back at the front. (While turning the bo over, keep it forward.) Finish this movement in kensei (for detailed photographs of this mochikae, refer to Figures 39–42).

The front tip of the bo and your line of sight still should project as one. Rest the back end of the bo lightly on your right upper arm.

31 Beginning the uchikomi, pull straight back on the bo from kensei.

32–33 Stepping forward with the right foot, in fudo-dachi, push the back part of the bo straight through with the right hand, striking forward and into chudan.

33 Finish in chudan stance. In this position, make sure that the lower hand (here, the left) keeps the bo resting lightly on the hip.

31   32   33

KENSEI

The term kensei refers to any of a number of ways of holding the bo so as to hold your opponent in check. In this book, however, the term is used only to refer to the position shown in Figure 30. In this kensei position, if your opponent approaches too closely, you can keep him back by jabbing him with the tip of the bo.

34

35

36

37

38

34 Left chudan stance: Stand in fudo-dachi with the left foot forward.

35–36 Mochikae and kensei. (Note that mochikae always needs to be done fast, so that you can move quickly from one technique to the next.) Draw the bo straight back in kensei.

37–38 Right jodan uchikomi: Uchikomi from jodan to chudan, while moving forward in fudo-dachi.

Mochikae when doing Jodan Uchikomi

39

40

41

42

39 Left chudan stance: Stand in fudo-dachi with the left foot forward.
40–42 Do mochikae and finish in kensei.

Daijodan uchioroshi

Uchioroshi from daijodan to chudan (Moving forward, fudo-dachi)

43

44

45

43 Right daijodan stance: Stand in fudo-dachi, with the left foot forward. Gripping the bo lightly, look far ahead, toward infinity. Holding the front end of the bo with your left hand, and the middle with your right hand, raise the bo directly overhead, with the back end slightly higher.

46

47

48

44–45 Right daijodan uchioroshi: While stepping forward with the right foot, in fudo-dachi, strike forward, bringing the bo down vertically in a large arcing motion.
46–48 Front views of Figures 43–45.

Jodan uchiharai

Uchiharai from jodan to chudan (Moving forward, fudo-dachi)

49

50

51

52

49 Jodan uchiharai stance: Stand in fudo-dachi, with the left foot forward. Hold the bo lightly and set your gaze far ahead. Hold the front of the bo with your left hand, and the middle with your right. The bo should be held diagonally, with its back end higher. Extend your left elbow forward.

50–52 Left jodan uchiharai: Stepping forward with the right foot, in fudo-dachi, cut diagonally down with the back end of the bo through chudan and, maintaining momentum, follow through to the left.

53

54

55

56

53–56 Front views of Figures 49–52.

Jodan gyaku-te uchi

Gyaku-te uchi from gedan to jodan (Moving forward, fudo-dachi)

57

58

59

60

57 Left chudan stance: Stand in fudo-dachi, with the left foot forward. (If you are practicing with a partner, point the bo at his throat.)
58 Pull back on the bo with your right hand.
59–60 Right gyaku-te uchi: While stepping forward with the right foot, in fudo-dachi, push the back end of the bo forward with your right hand, striking straight from gedan to jodan.

61

62

63

64

61–64 Front views of Figures 57–60.

Jodan uchikomi

Uchikomi from jodan to chudan (Kiba-dachi)

65

66

67

68

69

65 Left chudan stance: Stand in kiba-dachi, with your feet further apart than the width of your shoulders. The feet should be parallel, pointing forward.

66 Mochikae and kensei (switching hands and checking): Do mochikae and align the forward tip of the bo with your line of vision. Lightly rest the back end of the bo on your right upper arm. Your right elbow should be extended to the side.

67 Kensei: With your right hand, pull straight back on the bo, letting it slide into the position shown.

68–69 Right jodan uchikomi: Still in kiba-dachi, push the back end of the bo straight forward with your right hand, striking through into chudan.

70 71 72

73 74

70–74 Front views of Figures 65–69.

Suihei uchikomi

Uchikomi from chudan to chudan and gyaku-te uchi from chudan to chudan (Kiba-dachi)

75

76

77

78

While in kiba-dachi, practice uchikomi, hitting from chudan to chudan, and gyaku-te uchikomi—the same from the opposite side but without doing mochikae.

75 To begin, adopt kiba-dachi's left chudan stance. (If practicing with a partner, point the bo at his throat.)
76 Pull back on the back end of the bo with your right hand.
77–78 Right gyaku-te uchi: Push the back end of the bo straight forward with your right hand, striking through from chudan into chudan.

79

80

81

79 Pull back on the back end of the bo with your left hand.

80–81 Left chudan uchikomi: Push the back end of the bo straight forward with your left hand, striking through from chudan into chudan.

Practice right gyaku-te uchi and left chudan uchikomi many times, as a set; then do mochikae and practice the set from the other side as well.

82–88 Front views of Figures 75–81.

86   *87*

88

Jodan uchikomi

Uchikomi from jodan to chudan (Moving forward, musubidachi)

89   90

91   92

93   94

89 Left chudan stance: Stand in musubidachi. (If you are practicing with a partner, point the bo at his throat.)
90 Mochikae and kensei: Switch hands (mochikae) and hold your imagined opponent in check.
91 Draw the bo straight back.

95

96

97

98

99

100

92–94 Left jodan uchikomi: Taking a big step forward with the right foot, strike through with the back of the bo, pushing it straight into chudan with the right hand. As you complete this motion, draw your left foot up next to the right, into musubidachi.

95–100 Front views of Figures 89–94.

Matsukaze-uchi

Matsukaze-uchi followed by suna kake 1

101

102

103

101 Right chudan stance, fudo-dachi.
102–103 Rotate the bo counterclockwise, as if to draw a circle overhead with the front tip of the bo. At the same time, raise the right leg.

104 105
106 107

104–105 Continue rotating the bo.
106–107 With the front end of the bo, cut horizontally forward and through. While doing so, bring the right foot back to its original position.

Suna kake 1

(Kaze no kata version)

108

109

110

111

112

113

108 Point the front of the bo forward.

109–111 Rotate the bo vertically while raising the right foot.

112–113 Flick upward with the bottom of the bo.

In suna kake ("sand flicking") 1, the movement is of flicking sand from the ground into the face and eyes of your opponent. It occurs here in Figures 111–113. Figures 108–110 show the transition from matsukaze-uchi to suna kake 1.

114–116 Side views of Figures 111–113.

114

115

116

Suna kake 2

(Mizu no kata version)

117

118

119

SIDE VIEW

120

121

122

117 Stand on the left foot while resting the top of the right foot behind the left knee. With the left hand forward, hold your opponent in check.

118–119 Flick up with the back end of the bo.

120–122 Side views of Figures 117–119.

123   124   125

123–125 Back views of Figures 117–119.

TSUKIWAZA   Thrusting techniques

Chudan morote-zuki

(Moving forward, fudo-dachi, thrusting)

126

127

128

126 Left chudan stance, fudo-dachi.

127 Shifting the weight back into kokutsu-dachi, draw the bo back with both hands.

128 Thrust with the bo while taking a big step forward with the left foot.

ZENSHIN IPPON MOROTE-ZUKI

129

130

131

129 Left chudan stance, fudo-dachi.

130 With your left foot planted, cross your right foot past and well forward of it.
At the same time, draw back on the bo with both hands.

131 Thrust well forward, taking a big step with the left foot into fudo-dachi.

Chudan taguri-zuki

(Fudo-dachi)

132

133

134

132 Left chudan stance, fudo-dachi.

133 Shifting your weight back into kokutsu-dachi, draw back on the back part of the bo with your right hand, allowing the bo to slide through the left (front) hand. With the thumb of your left hand, conceal the head of the bo.

134 Taking a big step forward with the left foot, thrust the bo, fully extending it, as if you were piercing straight through an imagined target.

ZENSHIN IPPON TAGURI-ZUKI

135

136

137

135 Left chudan stance, fudo-dachi.

136 With the right foot, step past and well forward of the left foot. At the same time, draw back on the bo with the right hand, and allow the bo to slide through the left hand. Conceal the head of the bo with the thumb of the left hand.

137 Stepping through into fudo-dachi with the left foot, thrust forward with the bo, as if to pierce straight through an imagined target.

Gedan-barai with nukiotoshi

138
139
140

141
142
143

138 Left chudan stance, fudo-dachi.

139 With the right hand, draw the bo back.

140–141 Right gedan-barai: Stepping forward with the right foot into kokutsu-dachi, hit through gedan with the back part of the bo.

142–143 Nukiotoshi: With the left hand, pull up on the bo.
Still in kokutsu-dachi, let the bo drop down and through.

144   145   146

147   148   149

144–149 Front views of 138–143.

150

151

152

153

150 Right chudan stance, fudo-dachi.
151–156 While drawing a clockwise arc with the bo, shift your weight back into kokutsu-dachi.

154

155

156

157   158

159   160

157–163 Front views of Figures 150–156.

161

162

163

Ichimonji-uke

164

165

166

164 While in fudo-dachi, hold the bo horizontally with both hands, overhanded (with the backs of your hands facing up).

165–166 Stepping well back with your left foot, still in fudo-dachi, thrust the bo forward into daijodan.

167

168

169

167 Front view of Figure 166.
168–169 Practice this receiving motion in right jodan and left jodan as well.

170

171

172

170 Left chudan stance in fudo-dachi.

171–172 Pull the left foot in and then step forward into fudo-dachi again. At the same time, rotate the bo, bringing the forward tip down and the back end up. Push the bo forward.

173

174

175

173–175 Front views of Figures 170–172.

NOTES ON BASIC FORMS

FUDO-DACHI

176

177

178

179

180

181

176–177 Correct form: Note how the toes of the back foot point out to the side and a little to the front. The soles of the feet are firmly planted on the ground.

178–179 Incorrect form: The toes of the back foot are pointing backward.

180–181 Incorrect form: The bottom of the back foot is not planted properly.

JODAN UCHIKOMI

182

183

184

185

186

187

182 Correct form: While pulling back on the bo, keep the back elbow up, as shown.

183–184 Correct form: Bring the back hand straight through and forward as you do uchikomi.

185–187 Incorrect form: If you let your elbow drop (as here), you will be unable to strike straight through with the bo, and you will end up striking down, rather than straight through and forward.

GRIPPING THE BO

KENSEI

188   189

CHUDAN

190   191

188 Correct form.

189 Incorrect form: The grip on the bo is too tight here, and the elbows are held too low.

190 Correct form: Grip the bo lightly. Use the back hand to rest the bo on the hip.

191 Incorrect form: Don't grip the bo too tightly.

GRIPPING THE BO

KOHAN

192

MOROTE-ZUKI

193

KOHAN (IN NIDAN NO KATA)

194

MOROTE-ZUKI (IN NIDAN NO KATA)

195

192 With the front hand, be careful to roll the bo inward. Keep your back hand against your hip.

193 The front hand rotates outward as you thrust forward.

194–195 In Nidan no kata, kohan and morote-zuki (Chapter 6, Figures 53–54 and 65–66) are performed in a special manner. Both waza are done while cradling the bo, with the upper part of the back arm held against your ribcage.

CHAPTER 3

Kata

THE THREE BASIC KATA

Notes

The purpose of this chapter is to introduce three basic kata (set series of attack and defense movements) for the beginner. These kata are designed to make it easier for practitioners to learn more advanced kata (one of which will be introduced in Chapter 6). The kata shown here, which are simplified forms of these more difficult kata, incorporate the most important movements. They also contain elements of the basic practice exercises and techniques presented in Chapters 1 and 2. Each kata is complete and distinct in character. Each is high-level in terms of content but within the grasp of beginners.

(Please note that although the kata are shown here performed on the right side, they should be practiced on both sides.)

The three basic kata are:
• Hi no kata
Hi no kata is a condensed form of Nidan no kata, which is also known as Sakugawa no kon (and which will be shown in detail in Chapter 6).

• Kaze no kata
Kaze no kata is a condensed form of Sandan no kata, which is also referred to as Matsukaze no kon.

• Mizu no kata
Mizu no kata, which was developed by Master Fugaku Ito of Shintaido of America, is a condensed form of Yodan no kata, or Shirotaru no kon.

Hi no kata (Fire kata)

1 Begin in musubidachi (heels together, toes apart) with the bo in yoi (ready) position.

2 Aim the left end of the bo toward your imagined opponent's throat, keeping the opponent in check (kensei).

3 Pull the right end of the bo straight back.

4–5 Taking a step back with your left foot into fudo-dachi, strike forward as if to drive the bo into the opponent's shoulder at the base of the neck (jodan uchi).

6 Pull the left end of the bo back, sliding it through the right hand.

7   8   9

10   11   12

7–8 While taking a step forward with your left foot and keeping your weight back in kokutsu-dachi, sweep the left end of the bo through the opponent's gedan area (gedan-barai).

9 With the right hand, pull up on the bo, letting it slide diagonally through the left hand.

10 Controlling the bo with the right hand, let it drop quickly, sliding it through the left hand, toward the opponent's shin.

11–12 Stepping forward with the right foot into fudo-dachi, push the right end of the bo forward from below to receive a blow with ryuhi.

13   14   15

16   17   18

13–14 Still in fudo-dachi, rotate the left end of the bo down so that the bo is horizontal, to hold the opponent in check.

15 Drive the right end of the bo down into the base of the opponent's neck at the left shoulder (jodan uchikomi).

16–18 Shifting your weight back into kokutsu-dachi, receive the opponent's attack by drawing a large clockwise arc with the bo (kohan).

19   20   21

19–20 With kiai, thrust to your opponent's chudan area (morote-zuki) and assume fudo-dachi.

21 Draw your right foot back, next to your left foot, into musubidachi. This is yame position.

KIAI

Kiai is a sound that accompanies movement. It is usually a shout, but it can sometimes take the form of a cry or an exhalation of breath. Kiai is made when a technique is applied with one's whole being. It should, in principle, be made naturally and without intention, in relation to the body movement or technique.

Kaze no kata (Wind kata)

22 Stand in heisoku-dachi (with heels and toes together, touching) and assume yoi position.

23 While stepping forward with your left foot, point the left end of the bo diagonally upward, holding the imagined opponent in check.

24 Raise the right end of the bo overhead and behind you.

25 Step forward with your right foot into fudo-dachi, cutting forward broadly with the bo (daijodan uchioroshi).

26 Pull back on the bo with your left hand, letting it slide through the right hand.

27 Hit up from below with the left (back) end of the bo.

28

29

30

31

32

33

28 Hit down from above with the right end of the bo.

29 Hit up diagonally with the left end of the bo.

30 Hit with the right end of the bo (jodan uchikomi).

31–33 Swing the right end of the bo horizontally, counterclockwise, in a circle overhead and then around to the right. Raise and plant the right foot as you swing the bo (matsukaze-uchi).

34

35

36

37

38

39

34 Raise the right leg and, at the same time, bring the right end of the bo downward, into a vertical position.

35 While stepping forward with your right foot, bring the right end of the bo up in a scooping motion (suna kake 1).

36 Step forward with your left foot, passing it in front of the right foot, and pull the left end of the bo far back, letting it slide through the right hand. Use your right thumb to conceal the tip of the bo.

37 Step forward with your right foot while thrusting forward with the bo's right end (zenshin ippon taguri-zuki).

38 Slowly bring the bo back to chudan stance, fudo-dachi.

39 Draw your left foot forward, next to the right, in heisoku-dachi, assuming yame position.

Mizu no kata (Water kata)

40

41

42

43

40 In musubidachi (heels together, toes apart), assume yoi position.
41–42 Raise the right foot and rest it behind the left knee, while bringing the right end of the bo upward in a scooping motion (see Chapter 2, "suna kake 2").
43 While taking a big step forward with your right foot into fudo-dachi, thrust the bo with both hands into the opponent's chudan area (morote-zuki).

44 45 46

47 48

44–46 Shifting your weight back into kokutsu-dachi, receive the opponent's attack by drawing a wide clockwise arc with the bo (kohan).

47–48 Still in kokutsu-dachi, take a step forward with your left foot. At the same time, drive with the left end of the bo into the opponent's jodan area (gyaku-te uchi).

49

50

51

52

49–50 Draw your left foot back one step, into kokutsu-dachi. At the same time, defend your front jodan area (ryuhi).

51–52 Raise your right foot and, at the same time, swing the right end of the bo overhead and widely, counterclockwise. As you complete this motion, sweep the bo through the opponent's gedan area (matsukaze-uchi) and bring your right foot down.

53   54   55

56

57

53–54 Raise your right leg, resting the foot behind the left knee. At the same time, rotate the right end of the bo back and around again to the front, to hold the opponent in check.

55–56 From that position, rotate the bo, sweeping the right end from below in a scooping motion (suna kake 2).

57 Take a big step forward with your right foot into fudo-dachi, thrusting into the opponent's chudan area (morote-zuki).

58–60 Step forward with the left foot, passing in front of the right. While doing so, defend yourself by drawing a broad arc clockwise (kohan).

61 Take a big step forward with the right foot into fudo-dachi while thrusting into the opponent's chudan area (morote-zuki).

62 Draw your left foot next to your right, into musubidachi, assuming yame position.

CHAPTER 4

Basic and Applied Kumibo

GENERAL NOTES ON KUMIBO

The term kumibo refers to practice done with a partner, usually with bo striking bo. This chapter introduces both basic and applied kumibo.

In basic kumibo, decisions are made in advance about what techniques will be used for attacking and for receiving an attack. The two practice partners then set about sparring, one practicing basic attack moves, and the other, methods of receiving. Kumibo can be done even by beginners, as long as movements are kept to a slow pace. On the other hand, if the pace is quick and energetic, basic varieties of kumibo can present even advanced practitioners with a challenging keiko (practice session).

Even very advanced practitioners should go slowly at first and only increase their speed gradually; otherwise the bo can be very dangerous. Touching your partner even slightly with the bo can cause severe injury. The object of keiko is for all participants to improve their abilities, not to dominate or outdo one another.

With regard to applied kumibo, we will introduce the Shinjo sho kumibo kata, developed by Master Fugaku Ito of Shintaido of America. (There is a variation of Shinjo known as Shinjo dai, also developed by Ito-sensei, but this will not be introduced here.) Shinjo sho involves a continuous series of techniques, done in a realistic combative manner, alternating between offense and defense and providing ample practice in both.

Other forms of kumibo include free kumibo (in which two experienced practitioners spar without deciding on their methods in advance, freely changing their tactics throughout) and Soei kumibo (techniques that can be done either with a bo or with bare hands. Soei kumibo will be outlined in the next chapter).

Each of the exercises should be practiced repeatedly, without stopping. Partners should alternate roles and try both attacking and receiving many times.

It's also important that you enjoy yourself while doing these exercises.

1

2

3

Always begin kumibo with the following steps:

1 A (shown at left) and *B* (shown at right) stand in musubidachi and keep the bo tucked under their right arms (sage bo).

2 A and *B* bow to each other.

3 A and *B* complete their bow.

4

5

6

4 *A* and *B* bring the bo over to yoi position on the left side.

5 *A* and *B* hold each other in check (kensei).

6 *A* and *B* each draw their right feet back into fudo-dachi (chudan stance). They then move in closer together, to begin kumibo.

7

8

9

10

Always finish kumibo with the following steps:

7 Bring the feet together into musubidachi and then bring the bo over to the left side in yame position.

8 *A* and *B* return the bo to the right side (sage bo).

9 *A* and *B* bow to each other.

10 *A* and *B* face each other, concluding their kumibo.

> An attitude of respect for and gratitude to one another is essential. The practice of bowing to your partner before and after kumibo serves as a reminder of this principle.

BASIC KUMIBO

Jodan uchikomi attack received with jodan uchikomi

11

12

11 **A** and **B** both assume left chudan stance (fudo-dachi), with the bo lightly touching.
12 **A** and **B** do mochikae and kensei.

13

14

15

13 **A** steps forward with the right foot and attacks with right jodan uchikomi.
B steps backward with the left foot and receives using right jodan uchikomi.
14 **A** and **B** both do mochikae and kensei.
15 **A** steps forward with the left foot and attacks with left jodan uchikomi.
B steps backward with the right foot and receives with left jodan uchikomi.

Daijodan uchioroshi attack received with ichimonji-uke

16

17

16 *A* assumes left chudan stance (fudo-dachi).

B stands naturally, holding the bo with both hands overhand.

17 *A* does mochikae and assumes right daijodan stance.

B stands naturally.

18 *A* steps forward with the right foot while doing a right daijodan uchioroshi attack.

B pulls the left foot back into fudo-dachi, while doing ichimonji-uke in daijodan.

19 *A* does mochikae to hold the bo in left daijodan.

B stands naturally.

20 *A* steps forward with the left foot while attacking with left daijodan uchioroshi.

B steps back with the right foot into fudo-dachi while doing ichimonji-uke.

18

19

20

Jodan uchikomi attack received with ichimonji-uke

21

22

23

21 *A* and *B* both assume left chudan stance, with the bo lightly touching.

22 *A* does mochikae and kensei.

B slides the bo back with the back hand.

23 *A* steps forward with the right foot while attacking with right jodan uchikomi.

B pulls the left foot back while doing ichimonji-uke.

24

25

26

24 *A* assumes chudan stance.
B does mochikae.
25 *A* does mochikae and kensei.
B slides the bo back with the back hand.
26 *A* steps forward with the left foot while attacking with left jodan uchikomi.
B brings the right foot back while doing ichimonji-uke.

Gyaku-te uchi attack received with gyaku-te uchi

27

28

29

27 *A* and *B* assume left chudan stance, with the bo lightly touching.

28 *A* and *B* each slide their bo back with their back hands.

29 *A* steps forward with the right foot while attacking with right gyaku-te uchi.
B steps back with the left foot while receiving with right gyaku-te uchi.

30

31

32

30 *A* and *B* each do mochikae.
31 *A* and *B* each slide their bo back with their back hands.
32 *A* steps forward with the left foot while attacking with left gyaku-te uchi.
B steps back with the right foot while receiving with left gyaku-te uchi.

Gedan-barai attack received with gedan-barai

33

34

35

33 *A* and *B* assume left chudan stance (fudo-dachi), with the bo lightly touching.
34 *A* and *B* each slide their bo back with their back hands.
35 *A* steps forward with the right foot into kokutsu-dachi while attacking with right gedan-barai.
B steps back with the left foot into kokutsu-dachi while receiving with right gedan-barai.

36

37

38

36 *A* and *B* do mochikae and assume chudan stance (fudo-dachi).

37 *A* and *B* each slide their bo back with their back hands.

38 *A* steps foward with the left foot into kokutsu-dachi, while attacking with left gedan-barai.

B pulls the right foot back into kokutsu-dachi while receiving with left gedan-barai.

39

40

41

42

39 *A* and *B* assume right chudan stance (fudo-dachi), with the bo lightly touching.
40 *A* draws the bo back with both hands.
B begins shifting into kokutsu-dachi while beginning right kohan.
41–42 *A* attacks with right morote-zuki.
B traces a large arc with the bo in order to defend himself from *A*'s thrust: he catches *A*'s thrust and directs it over and down.

43

44

When you have learned to do steps 39–42, practice one of the counterattacks (either 43 or 44 below) that follow kohan:

43 **B** steps forward with the left foot into fudo-dachi and does left gyaku-te uchi to **A**'s face (for safety's sake, do not actually make contact). ***Alternatively,***
44 **B** steps forward with the right foot into fudo-dachi and does right morote-zuki to **A**'s chin (for safety's sake, do not actually make contact). (Note that here morote-zuki could alternatively be done to **A**'s middle area or right knee.)

(Be sure to practice kohan and the counterattacks on both the right and left sides.)

Morote-zuki attack received with ryuhi

45

46

45 *A* and *B* assume left chudan stance (fudo-dachi), with the bo lightly touching.
46 *A* draws the bo back with both hands.
B begins ryuhi.
47 *A* attacks with left morote-zuki .
B steps forward with the right foot and receives *A*'s attack with ryuhi.

When you have learned to do steps 45–47, practice the following counterattack:

48 *B* grabs *A*'s bo with the left hand and keeps it from moving, while putting his own bo in front of *A*.
49 *B* wedges his elbow (or bo) against *A*'s neck and bends him backward.

(Be sure to practice ryuhi and the counterattack on both the right and left sides.)

47

48

49

Yonhon kumibo (Kumibo featuring four kinds of attacks)

This form of kumibo involves practicing receiving four kinds of attacks in succession.

(1) Daijodan uchioroshi × ichimonji-uke
(2) Jodan uchikomi × jodan uchikomi
(3) Morote-zuki × kohan
(4) Gedan-barai × gedan-barai

50

51

50 *A* and *B* assume left chudan stance (fudo-dachi), with the bo lightly touching.
51 *A* does mochikae and assumes daijodan stance.
B readies the bo for ichimonji-uke.

52

53

54

52 *A* steps forward with the right foot, attacking with right daijodan uchioroshi.
B steps back with the left foot, receiving with ichimonji-uke.
53 *A* and *B* each do mochikae and kensei.
54 *A* takes a step forward with the left foot, attacking with left jodan uchikomi.
B steps back with the right foot, receiving with left jodan uchikomi.

55

56

55 *A* draws the bo back, preparing for morote-zuki.
B begins the arcing motion of kohan (in this case, counterclockwise), and begins to shift his weight into kokutsu-dachi.
56 *A* attacks with left morote-zuki.
B receives with kohan in kokutsu-dachi.

57

58

57 *A* and *B* each draw the bo back with their back hands.
58 *A* attacks with right gedan-barai, while stepping forward into kokutsu-dachi with the right foot.
B draws his left foot back into kokutsu-dachi while receiving with right gedan-barai.

(Be sure to practice yonhon kumibo on both the right and left sides.)

APPLIED KUMIBO

Shinjo sho

59

60

59 *A* and *B* assume left chudan stance (fudo-dachi), with the bo lightly touching.
60 *A* and *B* each do mochikae and kensei.

61

62

63

61 **A** steps forward with the right foot while attacking with right jodan uchikomi.
B draws the left foot back, receiving with right jodan uchikomi.
62 **A** and **B** each slide their bo back with their back hands.
63 **A** steps forward with the left foot while attacking with left gyaku-te uchi.
B pulls his right foot back while receiving with left gyaku-te uchi.

64

65

64 *A* raises the bo into daijodan.

B prepares to receive an overhead attack.

65 *A* steps forward with the right foot, doing right daijodan uchioroshi.

B changes his stance from left foot forward to right foot forward and meets *A*'s bo above and in front, right-handed.

66

67

66 *B* lightly deflects *A*'s attack, allowing *A*'s bo to pass downward to *B*'s right.
67 *B* swings the right end of the bo in a broad arc, diagonally and counterclockwise, sweeping through into gedan, finishing with arms crossed.
A meets *B*'s attack with left gedan-barai while switching his stance from right foot forward to left foot forward.

68

69

70

68–69 ***A*** holds the bo in kensei and, stepping forward with the right foot, attacks with right jodan uchikomi.

B turns the bo over end for end, pulls his right foot back and receives with left gyaku-te uchi, all in a single motion.

70–72 ***B***, while stepping forward with his right foot, sweeps his bo through and up, attacking with a scooping motion, and then immediately does right morote-zuki. ***A*** drops back and away from ***B***'s scooping attack and then receives ***B***'s morote-zuki with kohan.

71

72

73

74

73–74 *A* slides his bo back with his back hand and, stepping forward with the left foot, attacks with left gedan-barai.

B slides the bo back in the same manner and, stepping back with the right foot, receives with left gedan-barai.

75–77 *A* slides his bo back and steps forward with the right foot while attacking with a swinging blow to chudan (right suihei uchi).

B steps back with his left foot while doing ryuhi with the right end of the bo.

75

76

77

78

79

80

78–79 **A** again slides the bo back and thrusts with right taguri-zuki to gedan.
B swings the right end of his bo in a broad arc, diagonally and counterclockwise, receiving **A**'s attack in gedan.
80 **A** does mochikae while readying his bo in left daijodan.
B prepares to do ichimonji-uke.

81

82

81 *A* steps forward with the left foot while attacking with left daijodan uchioroshi. *B* steps back with the right foot while receiving *A*'s attack with ichimonji-uke.
82 *A* and *B* assume left chudan stance.

(Be sure to practice Shinjo on both the right and left sides.)

CHAPTER 5

Soei Kumibo

NAGEWAZA USED IN SOEI KUMIBO

The many nagewaza (throwing techniques) included in Shintaido bojutsu are gathered together in Soei kumibo. In this chapter we introduce some of these nagewaza.

Be sure to practice these techniques on both the right and left sides.

Throughout this chapter, instructions are given to direct blows to the head and torso of your opponent—in this case your partner in kumite. Practically speaking, you should never actually deliver a blow to any part of your practice partner's body, as doing so could too easily result in serious injury. Be conscious of your partner's safety.

Nagewaza Against Jodan Uchikomi
• Matoi-otoshi
• Sashikomi 1 (done from above the opponent's bo)
• Sashikomi 2 (done from below the opponent's bo)
• Sashikomi 3 (done from below the opponent's bo)
• Sashikomi 4 (done from below the opponent's bo)
• Uchi-muso
• Kaben-gaeshi
• Shoten
• Daisharin

Nagewaza Against Tsuki
• Daiheigen
• Matoi-otoshi
• Osoto-gari (using inside irimi)
• Osoto-gari (using outside irimi)
• Matoi-uchi
• Bear crush

NAGEWAZA AGAINST JODAN UCHIKOMI

Matoi-otoshi

1–2 **B** (shown at right) does right jodan uchikomi.

A (shown at left) meets **B**'s attack with ichimonji-uke (right hand underhand, left hand overhand).

3 **A** does outside irimi.

4–5 With the right hand, **A** grasps **B**'s bo to his own, then raises both bo high and thrusts down.

(For an explanation of irimi, see page 140.)

Sashikomi 1 (Done from above the opponent's bo)

6

7

8

9

10

6–7 As **B** attacks with right jodan uchikomi, **A** directs the left tip of his bo between **B**'s bo and body from above, next to **B**'s right wrist.

8 With the right end of the bo, **A** strikes **B** in the head or the side of the neck.

9–10 **A** places his bo against the base of **B**'s neck and pushes **B** over.

Sashikomi 2 (Done from below the opponent's bo)

11

12

13

14

15

11–12 As **B** attacks with right jodan uchikomi, **A** directs the left end of his bo under **B**'s oncoming bo and beyond **B**'s right shoulder.

13–15 **A** raises the right end of his bo and keeps it up while breaking **B**'s posture, making him fall backward.

Sashikomi 3 (Done from below the opponent's bo)

16

17

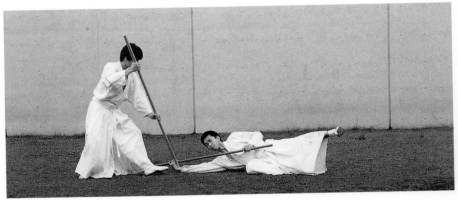

18

16 (Continuation of Figures 11 and 12.)
A wedges his bo behind *B*'s right wrist, from below.
17–18 *A* moves backward, pulling *B* off his feet.

Sashikomi 4 (Done from below the opponent's bo)

19   *A*   *B*

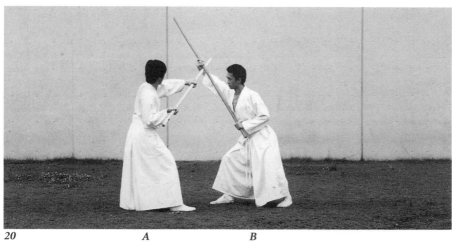

20   *A*   *B*

21   *B*   *A*

19 (Continuation of Figures 11 and 12.)
A wedges his bo behind *B*'s right wrist, from below.
20–21 *A* turns around, pulling *B* off his feet.

Uchi-muso

22   A   B

23   A   B

24   A   B

22–23 As *B* attacks with right jodan uchi, *A* does inside irimi.
24–27 With the right end of his bo, *A* scoops up *B*'s left leg and lifts, making *B* fall forward.

25   B   A

26   B   A

27   B   A

28

29

30

28–30 As **B** attacks with right jodan uchikomi, **A** does outside irimi, allowing **B** to pass. **A** punches **B** in the side with his right hand.

31

32

33

31–33 *A* places his left hand on *B*'s left shoulder and places his right hand against the back of *B*'s right knee, then pulls *B* over backward.

Shoten

34

35

34–35 As **B** attacks with right jodan uchikomi, **A** does inside irimi, passing his right hand under **B**'s bo.

36 **A** punches upward into **B**'s chin.

37–38 **A** then places the side of his open right hand against the base of **B**'s neck, at the shoulder, and pushes him over backward, with a forward cutting motion.

IRIMI

Integral to nagewaza is the concept of irimi. "Irimi" means entering a place close to your opponent that is both advantageous for striking him and safe from his attack. This chapter introduces inside irimi and outside irimi. Inside irimi refers to entering the space immediately in front of your attacking opponent. Outside irimi refers to entering the space immediately behind him.

36

37

38

39   *A*   *B*

40   *A*   *B*

41   *A*   *B*

39–41 As ***A*** attacks with right jodan uchikomi, ***B*** does inside irimi and takes hold of ***A***'s bo from below with both hands, as if to support his own.

42　　　　　　　　　　　　B　A

43　　　　　　　　　　　　B　　　　　　A

44　　　　　　　　　　　B　　　　　　　　A

42–44 While turning, **B** draws a big circle with both bo and uses **A**'s forward momentum to throw him.

NAGEWAZA AGAINST TSUKI

Daiheigen

45

46

47

48

49

50

45–46 As **B** attacks with right morote-zuki, **A** does outside irimi and receives the attack with ryuhi.

47 Using the left end of his bo, **A** holds **B** in check.

48–50 **A** applies the left end of his bo to the area under **B**'s chin. Then **A** moves his bo horizontally, pulling **B** over backward.

Matoi-otoshi

51

52

51–52 As *B* attacks with right morote-zuki, *A* does outside irimi, to receive with ryuhi.

53–55 Placing his bo against *B*'s left shoulder, *A* grips *B*'s bo to his own, then raises both bo high and thrusts down.

53

54

55

Osoto-gari (Using inside irimi)

56

57

58

59

60

61

56–57 As *A* attacks with right morote-zuki, *B* does inside irimi and receives *A*'s thrust with his bo.

58 *B* presses the right end of his bo into *A*'s neck.

59–61 With his right leg, *B* sweeps *A*'s right leg, sending *A* over backward.

Osoto-gari (Using outside irimi)

62

63

64

62–63 As *A* attacks with right morote-zuki, *B* receives it with kohan.
64 *B* does outside irimi to press the right end of his bo against *A*'s neck.

65

66

67

65–67 With his right leg, **B** sweeps **A**'s right leg, sending **A** over backward.

Matoi-uchi

68

69

68–69 As **B** attacks with right morote-zuki, **A** does outside irimi and places his left wrist with open hand under **B**'s chin.

70–72 **A** scoops up the bo with his open right hand into daiijodan, and then makes a fist with that same hand and strikes down into **B**'s face.

70

71

72

Bear crush

73

74

75

73–75 As ***B*** attacks with right morote-zuki, ***A*** does inside irimi and punches ***B*** under the chin.

76

77

78

76–78 With both hands, **A** grabs **B** by the head or the hair and pulls **B** down and toward him. **A** then thrusts his right knee up into **B**'s bo and face.

CHAPTER 6

Advanced Kata: Nidan no Kata

NIDAN NO KATA

The five major types of kata that have been established in Shintaido bojutsu are the first- through the fifth-dan kata, known as Shodan, Nidan, Sandan, Yodan and Godan no kata, in that order. Here we introduce Nidan no kata, which contains many kihon waza. Nidan no kata is based on the traditional kata Sakugawa no kon, which originated in Okinawa. It has been remade to reflect Shintaido theory and philosophy. Nidan no kata is an expansive, relaxed and beautiful kata.

1 Right sage bo (in seiritsu).
2 Right yoi position (heisoku-dachi).

3

4

5

6

3 Kensei (left end of bo forward).
4 Jodan uchikomi: Step back with the left foot into fudo-dachi while doing right jodan uchikomi.
5–6 Ryuhi.

7 Kensei (left end of bo forward).

8 Right jodan uchikomi.

9 Kohan: Using kohan, receive an attack in kokutsu-dachi.

10 Gedan-barai: Still in kokutsu-dachi, step forward with the left foot while doing left gedan-barai.

11–12 Nukiotoshi.

13 Ryuhi: Stepping forward with the right foot into fudo-dachi, do ryuhi.

14 Kensei (left end of bo forward).

15

16

17

18

15 Right jodan uchikomi.

16 Kohan (kokutsu-dachi).

17 Gedan-barai: Still in kokutsu-dachi, step forward with the left foot while doing left gedan-barai.

18 In fudo-dachi, hold the bo in daijodan, defending against an overhead attack.

19 As you drop into a very low kokutsu-dachi, hold down your imagined opponent's bo with the left end of your bo.

20–21 Nukiotoshi: Rise up into regular kokutsu-dachi and do nukiotoshi.

22 Kensei (left end of bo forward).

23

24

23 Jodan uchikomi: Stepping forward into fudo-dachi with the right foot, do right jodan uchikomi.

24 Ryuhi: Using your right foot as an axis, turn backward (counterclockwise) while doing ryuhi.

25

26

25 Pull the right foot back next to the left, into heisoku-dachi. This returns you to yoi position.

26 Gedan-barai: In kokutsu-dachi, step forward with the left foot while doing left gedan-barai.

27

28

27–28 Nukiotoshi.

29

30

29 Ryuhi: While stepping forward with the right foot into fudo-dachi, do ryuhi.
30 Kensei (left end of bo forward).

31

32

33

31 Right jodan uchikomi (fudo-dachi).

32 Kohan (kokutsu-dachi).

33 Stepping forward with the left foot (still in kokutsu-dachi), do gedan-barai.

34

35

36

34–35 Nukiotoshi.
36 Kensei (left end of bo forward).

37

38

39

37 Jodan uchikomi: Stepping forward with the right foot into fudo-dachi, do right jodan uchikomi.

38 Ryuhi: Using your right foot as an axis, turn backward (counterclockwise) while doing ryuhi (fudo-dachi).

39 Kensei (left end of bo forward).

40

41

42

40 Right jodan uchikomi.

41 Kohan (kokutsu-dachi).

42 Pull the right foot back next to the left into heisoku-dachi, and switch hands by sliding them on the bo (be sure to keep the bo on your left side).

43

44

45

46

43−44 Ryuhi: Do ryuhi while stepping to the left with the left foot, into fudo-dachi.
45 Kensei (right end of bo forward).
46 Left jodan uchikomi.

47

48

49

50

47 Hit up and through from below with the right end of the bo.

48 Left jodan uchikomi.

49–50 Gyaku-te uchi: Swing the right end of the bo over from behind and do right gyaku-te uchi.

51

52

53

54

51–52 Jodan uchikomi: Swing the left end of the bo over from behind and do left jodan uchikomi.

53 Kohan: While cradling the bo, with your right upper arm held against your ribcage, do kohan (kokutsu-dachi).

54 Morote-zuki: Still cradling the bo, do left morote-zuki (into fudo-dachi).

55

56

57

58

55 Mochikae: Do mochikae while drawing your right foot forward, into heisoku-dachi, and doing a quarter-turn to the right.

56 Ryuhi: Do ryuhi while stepping with the right foot into fudo-dachi.

57 Kensei (left end of bo forward).

58 Right jodan uchikomi.

59 Hit up and through from below with the left end of the bo.

60 Right jodan uchikomi.

61–62 Gyaku-te uchi: Swing the left end of the bo over from behind and do left gyaku-te uchi.

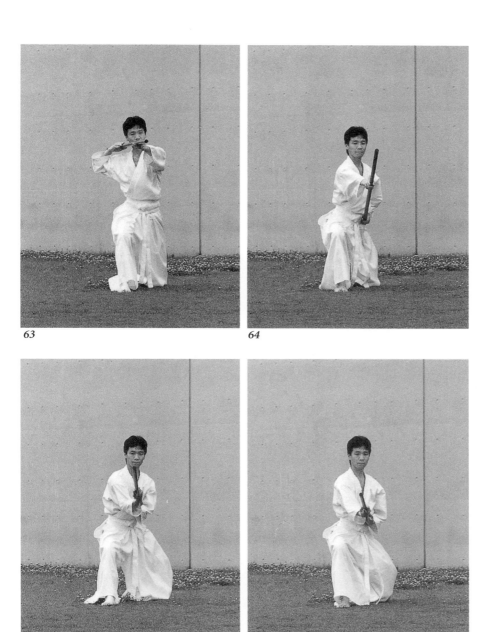

63
64
65
66

63−64 Swing the right end of the bo over from behind and do jodan uchikomi.
65 Kohan: While cradling the bo, with your left upper arm held against your ribcage, do kohan (kokutsu-dachi).
66 Morote-zuki: Still cradling the bo, do right morote-zuki (into fudo-dachi).

67

68

69

70

67 Gedan-barai: Keeping the right foot planted, step to the left into kokutsu-dachi while doing left gedan-barai.

68–69 Nukiotoshi.

70 Ryuhi: Stepping forward into fudo-dachi with the right foot, do ryuhi.

71

72

71 Kensei (left end of bo forward).
72 Right jodan uchikomi.

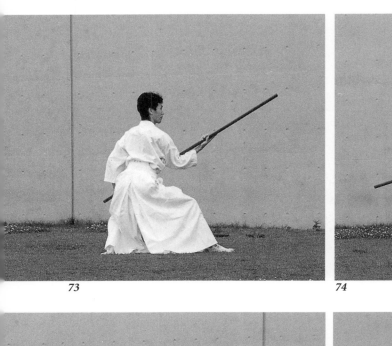

73

74

75

76

73 Kohan (kokutsu-dachi).
74–75 Right zenshin ippon morote-zuki (into fudo-dachi).
76 Kohan (kokutsu-dachi).

77

78

77–78 Right zenshin ippon morote-zuki (into fudo-dachi).

79 Kohan (kokutsu-dachi).

80–81 Right zenshin ippon morote-zuki (into fudo-dachi).

82 Kohan: Do kohan while stepping backward with the right foot, passing it in front of the left.

83

84

83 Kohan: Do kohan again while stepping back with the left foot (kokutsu-dachi).
84 Kohan: Do kohan again while stepping back with the right foot, passing it in front of the left (kokutsu-dachi).

85

86

87

85 Keeping the left foot planted and, stepping sideways with the right into kiba-dachi, hit with the left end of the bo into chudan (suihei uchi).

86 Still in kiba-dachi, hit with the right end of the bo into chudan (suihei uchi).

87 Take a step forward with the right foot into fudo-dachi.

88

89

90

91

88–89 While stepping forward with the left foot, passing it in front of the right, draw the bo back with both hands and thrust forward.

90–91 While stepping forward with the right foot into fudo-dachi, draw the bo back and thrust forward.

92

93

94

95

92 Turn 180° to the left.

93 Kensei: While holding your imagined opponent in check, rise up.

94 Raise the bo into right daijodan.

95 Daijodan uchioroshi: Stepping forward with the right foot (into fudo-dachi), do right daijodan uchioroshi.

96

97

98

99

96 Mochikae: Do mochikae and raise the bo into left daijodan.
97 Daijodan uchioroshi: Stepping forward with the left foot, do left daijodan uchioroshi.
98 Mochikae: Do mochikae and raise the bo into right daijodan.
99 Daijodan uchioroshi: Stepping forward with the right foot, do right daijodan uchioroshi.

100–101 Gedan-barai: Keep the right foot planted and step out sideways with the left foot into kiba-dachi, doing left gedan-barai.
102–103 Nukiotoshi (kiba-dachi).

104–105 Ryuhi: Still in kiba-dachi, turn your torso 180°, doing ryuhi.
106–107 Gedan-barai: Stepping forward with the left foot into kokutsu-dachi, do left gedan-barai.

108

109

108–109 Nukiotoshi.

110

111

112

113

110 Ryuhi: Turn 180° into fudo-dachi, doing ryuhi (fudo-dachi).

111 Kensei (left end of bo forward).

112 Right jodan uchikomi.

113 Kohan (kokutsu-dachi).

114

115

114 Yame: Drawing the right foot back into heisoku-dachi, stand in right yame position.
115 Right sage bo (seiritsu).

CHAPTER 7

Tenshingoso and Meditation

ON TENSHINGOSO

Tenshingoso and Eiko stand as the great foundation of Shintaido. It is this dual foundation from which keiko develops and to which it returns.

Eiko is a kata concerned with the themes of god, psychology, ideals, desire and prayer. In addition it is a way to break out of the isolation of one's ordinary existence, and to discover a larger, more open world. This kata is most basically done without a weapon, open-handed. But in Shintaido bojutsu it is studied in the forms of Bo no ageoroshi and Eiko dai with bo (refer to pages 22 and 24).

On the other hand, Tenshingoso is a kata concerned with the theme of the self. The word "Tenshin" refers to that truth which is the origin of the universe, and it also refers to the true form of the self without any pretense or affectation, and so has a sense of great serenity and freedom.

In Shintaido, "Tenshin" is the same thing that is referred to in other traditions as, for instance, "nature," "nothingness," "emptiness," "the Way," "Heaven," "God," "the Buddha" or "the Creator."

The word "goso" comes from esoteric Buddhism. The central figure in esoteric Buddhism is the godhead Dainichi Nyorai, who is considered to be the origin of the universe. The five sightings, or appearances, of Dainichi Nyorai—the center and true nature of the universe—are known as "goso."

The word "goso" in "Tenshingoso" is not understood to mean a group of five different forms, but rather an endless cycle of alternating forms.

When people become their original true selves, without any impurities or anything unnecessary, they become one with that which is called "god" and which is the original truth and the center of the universe. "Tenshingoso" actually refers to the ways in which these "selves which have become themselves" undergo various changes and appear and move. In other words, "Tenshingoso" refers to the everchanging universe, to the self, and to the worlds in flux that these create.

From the technical perspective of martial arts, there are a great many uchiwaza, ukewaza and nagewaza contained within Tenshingoso. It contains between ten and twenty well-known kata, and if these are broken down into more specific movements, there is virtually no limit to their number.

Tenshingoso should not be viewed as a collection of separate movements at all. Do keiko thinking of Tenshingoso as one large, fluid motion.

TENSHINGOSO (SEI: FORMAL)

Tenshingoso is usually done while vocalizing five sounds. These are "AH," "EH," "EE," "OH" and "UN."

UN, which is said at both the beginning and end of the kata, is pronounced deeply, focusing on the N, so that the sound reverberates to your very core. AH, EH, EE and OH are said out loud in a strong voice. Each of the five syllables should be held for the time it takes to exhale one full breath.

A person's ability, character and potential are all expressed when doing Tenshingoso. For instance, it is likely that a passive, withdrawn person whose ability to actively improve his own life and achieve his own potential is weak will have a weak EH movement and sound. A person who lacks experience in teaching and guiding others will probably be weak in EE. And someone lacking in generosity or the capacity for harmony will lack depth in the OH movement and sound.

On the other hand, if Tenshingoso functions as a diagnostic kata that shows the self as it presently is, it also serves as a kata for developing and drawing out unrealized areas of the self.

In keiko individuals should focus on the points that they consider to be their own weaknesses. That is, someone who is passive may want to focus on EH, someone who lacks leadership ability might practice EE, and someone who wants to be a more generous person may wish to focus on OH.

If you properly understand all the movements included in Tenshingoso, and strive to learn to do each movement correctly, you will find that the strength that you thought you lacked was actually dormant within you, and you will notice it beginning to develop and take shape.

(As you read, please note that this chapter's instructions are meant as a simple guide and should not strictly dictate or limit your ideas as you experience Tenshingoso.)

Vocalization of UN

1

1 Place your feet side by side, touching, as in heisoku-dachi. Wrap your right hand lightly around the thumb of your left hand, and gently enclose the fingers of your right hand in your left hand. Your eyes can either be half-closed or lightly closed. You may tilt your head slightly forward.

Stand with your weight slightly forward and your lower back relaxed and slightly back.

Vocalize UN, allowing the 'N' sound to reverberate through your body to its core.

Lower your consciousness to the depths of the earth and return to a state of serenity (without thinking or feeling anything).

UN involves the darkness of the chaos we knew before our birth, the state of non-being, and freedom from all ideas and thoughts. It returns us to our origins, and gives us a sense of depth and calm.

Vocalization of AH

2

3

4

2–4 While vocalizing AH, open your eyes and place your right foot one step to the side, so that your legs are a little wider than the width of your shoulders. Stand with your toes pointing outward. You may raise them off the ground.

As you do the above, open your hands, thrusting out from the center of your palms. Keep the fingers stretched back and as wide apart as possible.

Keeping your arms extended, bring them backward, past your hips and behind you.

Allow yourself to arch slightly backward and let your arms arc behind as you gradually raise them. Shift your gaze upward.

(Avoid becoming overly enthusiastic, stretching too far or moving too suddenly.)

5

6

7

8

5–8 As you raise your arms, keep the palms of your hands facing more or less outward. Stretch your whole body toward the sky, thrusting the center of your palms upward. As your arms come together, the wrists should face each other.

With your eyes wide open, look deep into the heavens.

AH involves birth, trust and the blessings of nature. It brings growth, praise and a spirit of journeying or seeking. It involves entrusting yourself completely to nature and to growth by losing yourself. Open your heart and body as you look upward and stretch your hands up. As you extend, think of yourself as stretching toward your dreams and ideals. When you have stretched your hands to their limit, extend them still further as if you were either receiving something from heaven or continuing to reach for something.

Vocalization of EH

9

10

9–10 Move your upraised hands closer together and twist them, bringing the thumbs forward while keeping the little fingers close together.

> Throughout Tenshingoso, be sure to keep your hands wide open by thrusting out from the center of your palms. In this position your wrists are cocked back and your fingers are spread as wide open as possible. Also note that in AH, your visual focus is heavenward. In EH through OH it is forward. In all these cases it is infinite.

11

12

13

14

11–14 While vocalizing EH, use the whole length of your arms to cut forward and diagonally, keeping your shoulders relaxed and your elbows slightly bent. Imagine yourself cutting open whatever is blocking your way. Set your visual focus infinitely forward.

EH involves crystallization and breaking new ground. Crystallize all praise with your dreams and ideals. Then realize your dreams and ideals with the strength of your resolve. Break new ground and begin to cultivate the rest of of your life for yourself. Share what you have been given with others.

Vocalization of EE

15

16

17

18

15–18 Draw your hands to the sides of your hips. While vocalizing EE, press with your hands at first slightly downward and then gradually forward, as if you were heaping something up in front of you. Gradually extend your arms forward until your thumbs and index fingers almost touch. The opening between your hands will outline a small triangle. Look forward infinitely through this opening as you push out from the center of your palms.

EE involves collection, direction, leadership, cultivation of will. EE increases your ability to grasp the situation at hand, to take responsibility and to gather, guide and educate people. Spread your hands as wide as possible and clarify your existence. Cultivate self-confidence and resolve.

Vocalization of OH

19

20

21

22

19–26 While vocalizing OH, arc your arms behind you. Allow your arms to take in all that is around you. Do this while keeping your weight slightly forward. Continue moving your arms down and gradually forward, as if to embrace what is before you. Stretch forward, bringing your hands together side by side, palms forward, fingers pointing down. Look beyond your hands as you raise them above the horizon.

OH involves flowering, love, broad-mindedness, offering, consecration, and the whole of creation. It encompasses all of creation, brings it to fruition and offers all up to the heavens. This gives people true grandeur and gentleness.

23

24

25

26

Vocalization of UN

27

28

27–30 Vocalize UN as you place your right hand into the palm of the left, and bring both hands down just below your chest. At the same time, bring your right foot next to the left. While further lowering the hands, wrap the fingers of the right hand lightly around the left thumb, and wrap the fingers of the left hand lightly around the right hand. Return the hands to their original position.

UN marks a return to the beginning. UN seeks to offer up everything to God and to heaven and earth. It embodies a return to the earth. It leads to a place of humility that offers a clear vision of one's own life.

Doing Tenshingoso is an appropriate way to begin and end keiko.

29

30

MEDITATION

Sit or stand comfortably in a correct posture, regulating your breathing and quieting your mind. This will allow you to directly observe your real self.

There are various thoughts on the question of what position is best for meditation, but when you first start out, try either of the positions described here—seiza (Figures 31–36) or seiritsu (refer to Figure 46). The object is eventually to get to the point where you can reach a deep meditative state even while you are performing any of the bojutsu kata.

By becoming at one with the life energy of the universe (ki), you can awaken your consciousness and free your spirit. Meditation, correctly done, will help you to do so.

In order to achieve a quiet and profound sense of humanity, begin by practicing meditation fifteen minutes a day, and gradually increase the amount to about forty-five minutes to one hour a day.

Seated meditation (Ki-itsu-i; return to oneness)

31 32 33

34   35

36

31–36 Begin by bowing. These figures illustrate a particular way of bowing that is done before meditation and that prepares the mind and body for entering a meditative state.

First, kneel while keeping your upper body relaxed but straight (shown in Figures 31 and 34). Rest your hands, palms down or up, on your thighs, release any tension from your shoulders, and face straight ahead. Keep your knees about the width of one or two fists apart.

Your feet should be close enough together that the big toe of each foot are lightly touching.

What to do with your eyes is up to you. There are three choices: you can open them gently and look toward infinity, or half-close them and look slightly downward. Or you may keep them gently shut.

Bow. Bring the fingers of both hands together and lean forward until you touch the ground in front of you (Figures 31–33 and 34–36). Keep your spine straight as you lean forward.

Return to seiza (Figures 31 and 34).

Take a deep breath, slowly. Hold it for a count of four, then slowly release. Repeat once more.

The following is a way of relieving the tension that tends to settle in the head, neck, shoulders and stomach:

Little by little, release the tension, fatigue, mental inflexibility and weight of gravity from your head downward. Imagine releasing all these burdens, lowering them from your head to your neck, from your neck to your shoulders, from your shoulders to your chest, from your chest to your stomach, from your stomach to your abdomen, from your abdomen to your perineum, from your perineum to the ground, and finally to the depths of the earth.

Repeat this process, which is called "lowering your center of gravity."

Repeat once more, this time stopping the center of gravity at your perineum. Be still and wait for the ki of heaven and earth to fill your body.

Bow again to bring this exercise to a close.

Standing meditation

Spread your feet to about the width of your shoulders, and stand straight, in sei-ritsu (refer to Figure 46). Let your hands hang at your sides. Release all tension from them. Face straight ahead, and half-close your eyes and look slightly downward, or lightly close your eyes.

Stand with your koshi slightly back and your weight just forward of the arches of your feet.

Little by little, release the tension, fatigue, mental inflexibility and weight of gravity from your head downward. Imagine lowering all these burdens from your head to your neck, from your neck to your shoulders, from your shoulders to your chest, from your chest to your stomach, from your stomach to your lower abdomen, from your abdomen to your perineum, from your perineum to the ground, and finally to the depths of the earth.

Repeat this process.

Then repeat once more, this time stopping the center of gravity at the soles of your feet. Do not let the ki leave the soles of your feet.

Increasing your powers of concentration

Continuing this exercise for two or three months will greatly increase your powers of concentration.

Draw a circle two to three millimeters in diameter on a piece of paper and fix the paper to the wall.

Position yourself one to two meters away from the paper. Gaze at the circle.

Continue gazing at the circle for fifteen to thirty minutes.

If you continue doing this exercise regularly for one to three weeks, you will eventually find that the size of the circle seems to increase, to about one meter in diameter.

The following steps all need to be done with your imagination.

Draw a horizontal line, through the middle of the one-meter circle, from one edge of the circle to the other.

At the end of that line place a circle about one centimeter in diameter.

Try adding another circle next to the one you just envisioned.

Continue adding circles until you have one hundred lined up. Then select one from about the middle of the line, and gaze at it until it expands to one meter. Repeat the entire sequence.

Finally, change the exercise this way: Of the one hundred black circles, leave only one at about the center.

Practice piercing this last circle with the bo.

Ritsui-ju meiso-ho (Ten stages of standing meditation)

37

38

39

40

41

37 Stage 1: Muso-i (Nothingness)
38 Stage 2: Hoko-i (Spreading light)
39 Stage 3: Seiji shosei-i (Brightening world)
40 Stage 4: Tencho-i (Top of heaven)
41 Stage 5: Kongo gassho-i (Diamond)

42

43

44

45

46

42 Stage 6: Kenka-i (Offering flowers)
43 Stage 7: Dai kenka-i (Offering the body)
44 Stage 8: Bokyo-i (Looking homeward)
45 Stage 9: Joshin-i (Clearing the mind)
46 Stage 10: Kiitsu seiritsu-i (Oneness; returning to being)

APPENDICES

THE GREATER STRUCTURE OF SHINTAIDO

The Relationships Among Different Areas of Keiko

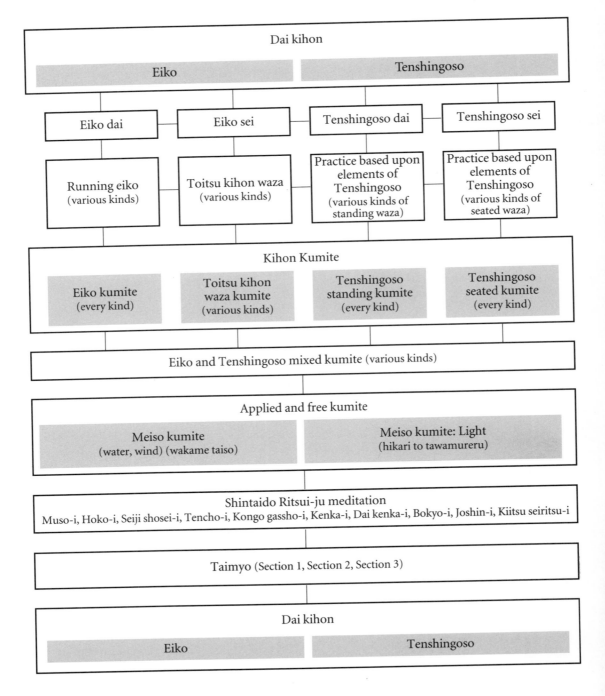

The Relationships Among Various Fields of Shintaido

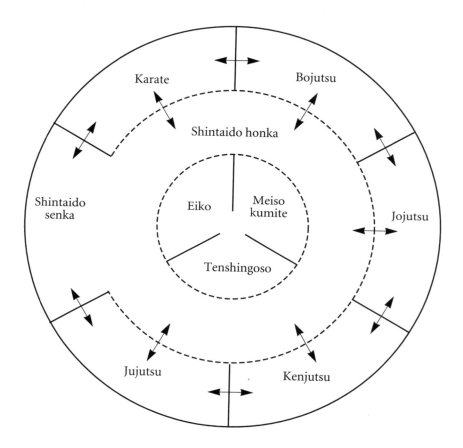

Karate

Bojutsu

Shintaido honka

Shintaido senka

Eiko

Meiso kumite

Jojutsu

Tenshingoso

Jujutsu

Kenjutsu

A LOOK AT DAIJODAN, JODAN, CHUDAN AND GEDAN

Daijodan

Jodan

Chudan

Gedan

STANCES: FOOT POSITIONS

Heisoku-dachi   Musubidachi   Hachiji-dachi (seiritsu)

Fudo-dachi   Kiba-dachi

MOVING IN MUSUBIDACHI
(Stepping practice for attack and defense)

The patterns shown here are basic and essential forms of stepping practiced in
Shintaido. These patterns are seen particularly in kumibo and Soei kumibo, so
students are recommended to practice them until they achieve mastery.

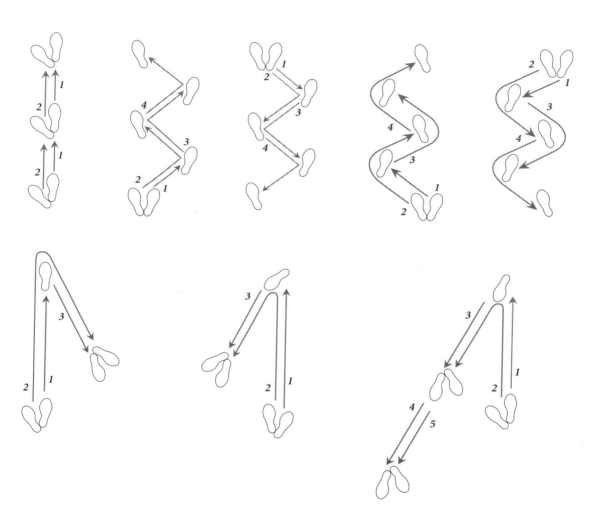

(NOTE: All of these forms of practice can also be done with the positions of the feet
reversed left for right.)

SHINTAIDO POINTS OF CONTACT

Japan
SHINTAIDO KYOKAI
Shinmei Building, 1–16–9 Shiba-Daimon, Minato-ku, Tokyo 105–0012
Tel. (+813) 5401–1167
Fax (+813) 5401–1168
E-mail: mail@shintaido.com
Home page: http://shintaido.com/

U.S.A.
SHINTAIDO OF AMERICA
E-mail: info@shintaido.org
Home page: http://shintaido.org/

U.K.
SHINTAIDO FOUNDATION
E-mail: jeffulachambers@mistral.co.uk

France
PIERRE QUETTIER
E-mail: quettier@multimania.com

Italy
GIANNI ROSSI
E-mail: rossig@micanet.it
Home page: http://www.shintaido.it/

For more information, visit:
Home page: http://shintaido.com/totalstickfighting/

GLOSSARY

Bo balancing: Exercises in which the bo is balanced on the body in a variety of ways

Bo juggling: Exercises in which the bo is spun in a variety of ways

Bo no ageoroshi: Exercise in which the bo is repeatedly raised and lowered from an outstretched horizontal position (shoko) to an outstretched vertical position (tenso)

Bojutsu: Wooden staff techniques

Budo: Japanese martial arts, or, literally, the martial Way

Catch-bo: Exercise in which the bo is thrown into the air and caught either between partners or alone

Chudan: Middle level

Cut: Manner of striking in which the bo is driven or swung through and beyond its immediate target. The focus of such an attack includes and extends beyond the immediate target

Dai: Large; greater

Daijodan: Uppermost level; overhead

Dan: Level of waza (in regard to elevation)

Eiko 栄光 (Lit., "glory"): One of the fundamental movements of Shintaido

Fudo-dachi (Lit., "immovable stance") Way of standing in which the knees are bent and the feet are set wider than shoulder width, one foot pointing forward and the other pointing to the side; body weight is distributed evenly between the two feet

Furimawashi: Exercise in which one or more bo are held at their end and swung horizontally back and forth around the body

Gasshuku: Retreat workshop

Gedan: Lower level

Gyaku: Opposite; reverse

Gyaku-te uchi: Opposite-hand strike (little finger forward)

Hachiji-dachi: Way of standing in which the feet are set naturally at about shoulder width

Harai (barai): Wielding the bo with a sweeping motion, as if with a sword

Heisoku-dachi: Stance in which the feet are placed flatly together, touching at the heels and toes

Hi no kata (Lit., "fire kata"): A basic kata of Shintaido bojutsu

Hitori-geiko: Solitary practice

Hoshi-otoshi (Lit., "making stars fall"): Basic exercise done with the bo held vertically, as in tenso

Ichimonji-uke 一文字受け: Blocking technique in which the bo is thrust or swung with both hands upward or to the side to receive a blow at its middle

Ippon: In the context of bojutsu technique, one thrust

Irimi 入り身 (Lit., "entering body"): Entering a place close to your opponent that is both advantageous for striking him and safe from his attack. Inside irimi refers to entering the space immediately in front of your attacking opponent. Outside irimi refers to entering the space immediately behind him.

Irimukae 入り迎え (Lit., "entering and inviting in"): Basic exercise that promotes a sense of oneness with the bo

Jo: Short staff (about 130 centimeters or slightly less)

Jodan: Upper level

Jojutsu: Short staff techniques

Jujutsu: Traditional techniques for grappling and throwing

Kamae: Stance; position

Kata: Series of formal attack and defense movements

Kaze no kata (Lit., "wind kata"): A basic kata of Shintaido bojutsu

Keiko: Practice or training

Ken: Sword

Kenjutsu: Sword techniques

Kensei: Stance in which the opponent is held in check with the bo

Kiai: Sound made to accompany movement, commonly in the form of a shout

Kiba-dachi (Lit., "horse-riding stance"): Stance in which the knees are bent and the feet are set parallel and apart, wider than shoulder width

Kihon: Basis; foundation

Kohan 虎翻: Ukewaza in which the bo is moved in a circular fashion in front of the body

Kokutsu fudo-dachi (Also referred to simply as kokutsu-dachi or kokutsu): Fudo-dachi stance in which the weight distributed mainly over the back foot

Koshi: The area of the body where the hips and waist meet

Kumibo 組棒: Partner practice using bo; sparring with bo

Meiso: Meditation

Mizu no kata (Lit., "water kata"): A basic kata of Shintaido bojutsu

Mochikae: Switching from holding the bo right-handed to left-handed and vice versa; exercise in which this is practiced

Morote-zuki: Tsukiwaza in which the bo is thrust without sliding it through the hands

Musubidachi: Stance in which the feet are placed together, heels touching, toes apart, in a "V" shape

Nage: A throw; throwing

Nagewaza: Throwing techniques

Namigaeshi 波返し (Lit., "turning back waves"): Exercise for practicing receiving repeated thrust attacks from the front

Ritsui-ju meiso-ho 立位十瞑想法: Ten positions of standing meditation

Ryuhi 龍飛: Ukewaza in which the bo is held outward to receive a blow

Sage bo: Position for standing at ease with the bo

Sanpo-uke 三方受け: Exercise for practicing receiving overhead attacks from three directions (left, right and center), using ichimonji-uke

Sei: Formal, correct

Seiritsu 正立: Formal/correct standing style in which the feet are placed at shoulder width, as in hachiji-dachi

Seiza: Formal/correct sitting style

Sensei: Teacher

Shinjo 真常: A Shintaido bojutsu kumibo kata for two practitioners

Shintaido honka: Shintaido core curriculum

Shintaido senka: Advanced Shintaido

Sho: Small; lesser

Shoko 証光: Position in which the bo is extended horizontally toward the horizon

Soei kumibo 創営組棒: Kumibo involving nagewaza

Suna kake (Lit., "flicking sand"): Technique for distracting or impairing the vision of an opponent by flicking sand or dirt into his face

Taguri-zuki: Tsukiwaza in which the bo is slid through the forward hand

Taiso: Exercises

Ten-nage (Lit., "throwing to heaven"): Catch-bo practiced alone

Tenshingoso 天真五相: One of the fundamental movements of Shintaido

Tenso 天相: Position in which the bo is extended vertically toward heaven

Tsuki (zuki): A thrust; a jab; a punch; thrusting; jabbing; punching

Tsukiwaza: Thrusting techniques

Uchi: A hit; a blow; striking

Uchiharai: Striking by swinging through

Uchikomi: Striking into, striking through

Uchioroshi: Striking down; striking by lowering

Uchiwaza: Striking techniques

Uke: To receive; receiving. In the context of bojutsu, "uke" refers to receiving an attack

Ukewaza: Technique for receiving attacks

Waza: Techniques

Yame: "Stop" [command commonly heard during keiko]

Yoi: "Ready" [command commonly heard during keiko]

Zenkutsu fudo-dachi (Also referred to as zenkutsu or zenkutsu-dachi): Fudo-dachi stance with the body weight distributed mainly over the front foot

Zenshin: (1) Moving forward. (2) Whole body

Additional useful terms

Ato no e: Back part of the bo

Bo bi: Tail of the bo

Bo taiso: Warm-up exercises (done with the bo)

Bo to: Head of the bo

Gorei: Leading of keiko

Hajime: "Begin" [command commonly heard during keiko]

Hon-te uchi: Normal uchikomi strike (using a conventional grip, with the index finger of the front hand forward)

Kohai: Practitioner who began studying after you

Kotai: Stepping back

Matsukaze 松風 (Lit., "pine wind")

Matsukaze-uchi: A swinging strike (seen in Kaze no kata and Mizu no kata)

Naka no e: Middle part of the bo

Nukiotoshi: Downward poke or thrusting movement

Saki no e: Front part of the bo

Senpai: Practitioner who began studying before you

Ushiro e: "Turn around" [command commonly heard during keiko]

Yasume: "Rest" (command commonly heard during keiko)